AUSTRALIAN BUSHCRAFT

AUSTRALIAN ARMY EDUCATION
SERVICE

1942

Name: _Jade Sanchez Melton_

Rank: ———————————

Army Number: ———————

Unit: ———————————

AUSTRALIAN
BUSHCRAFT

AUSTRALIAN ARMY EDUCATION SERVICE

AUSTRALIAN BUSHCRAFT

ISBN-13: 978-1475223118
ISBN-10: 1475223110

Printed in U.S.A

CONTENTS:

Page

CHAPTER 1.—Making a Fire   7

CHAPTER 2.—Getting Water   13

CHAPTER 3.—Developing an Eye for Coun-
try   24

CHAPTER 4.—Food   26

CHAPTER 5.—Miscellaneous Hints   40

Note:

The author of this booklet is a member of the AA Education Service.

The booklet has a double purpose. It is meant to follow up the practical work in bushcraft done under AA Education Service instruction. It should also satisfy a general demand for information on this subject.

INTRODUCTION

THERE is nothing mysterious about bushcraft; anyone with average intelligence can master it if he puts his mind to it. The exception is tracking; to do that properly you have to be trained from infancy, and keep in practice, too, throughout your life.

Contrary to what most people think, native races do not possess powers denied to civilised man; if they can do a thing, so can we, and a grounding in the sciences helps us to beat them at their own game, because we then know the why and the wherefore of things and do not have to rely on blind belief alone. From the outset, therefore, the bushcraft student should begin his studies with the idea firmly fixed in his mind that he is not going to be shown dark and deadly secrets, but will merely be taught a lot of dodges and tricks whose main feature is their very simplicity.

The correct mental approach to a lesson is very important. You can be prepared for lessons both interesting and useful. some exercises which call for patience, a retentive memory and a fair degree of manual dexterity; above everything else, you will be called upon to use your powers of observation to the limit. But there will be nothing mysterious.

There are two ways of learning bushcraft, and you can make your choice now — the easy way and the hard way. The hard way is to wait until some emergency arises and then try to put into practice the hints given on these pages; the easy way is to get in the necessary practice now so that the emergency finds you fully skilled. It is a sad fact that most men who receive the kindergarten lessons in bushcraft never do anything more in regard to acquiring skill in all the little tricks; let an emergency arise and they will probably prove how dangerous a thing a little knowledge can be. Some, however, take up the work with enthusiasm, practise the stunts at every opportunity, and so gain that steady confidence in their own ability which can be such a priceless asset to the man who suddenly finds himself cut off from all the advantages of civilisation.

The skilled bushman is not only a great asset to the fighting forces of his own country; he is also the type of soldier who is hardest to kill. By studying bushcraft you really take out one of the best of all insurances against losing your life.

Chapter One

MAKING A FIRE

WE shall start with the art of firemaking without matches. All native races know how to do it; but take away a box of matches from the average civilised man and he is at a loss. Yet it isn't hard to pick up the knack; boy scouts have lit fires without matches in less than 40 seconds.

The simplest and most convenient method is to use a box of tinder and flint and steel. To make your tinder box take an ordinary boot polish tin, scour the inside with sand or ashes until it is quite bright and free from all traces of grease. For tinder take a piece of clean, dry cotton rag about 18 inches long and 4 inches wide. Place the tinder tin on the ground with the lid off; hold your strip of rag over a fire by means of a couple of sticks; let it scorch first by holding it out of the reach of the flame, then let it take fire. Just as the last of the flame dies from the strip of rag and it is glowing red, lower it into the tin, folding it with a to-and-fro motion of the sticks, and then clamp the lid on.

This shuts out the air and extinguishes the glowing cotton; when the tin is cold remove the lid and inside you'll see a heap of black, brittle flakes. Those flakes are tinder — actually, carbon in a very finely divided state — bone dry and ready to catch fire when the smallest spark falls on it. In damp climates keep your tinder dry by putting a strip of adhesive tape around the edge of the tin, and never keep the tin open longer than is necessary.

If you haven't any rag you can use kapok, bamboo or reed pith, the fungus which grows on tree trunks, and rotting logs, or, dry fluff from the base of a zamia palm. Whatever it may be, dry it thoroughly; rub it into fluff or small chips, char it on a bit of tin which has been heated over a fire or on a stone which has been heated; as soon as it is glowing redly all through, transfer it quickly to the tin and put the lid on.

7

True flint is comparatively rare in Australia, but that doesn't matter because there are numerous substitutes. Quartz is the commonest, but you can also use any of the glassy stones which are too hard to be scratched by a steel point — chert, rock crystal, topaz, or even a rock-like granite if it has small, hard crystals such as quartz or garnet, embedded in it. Try the various stones out in the dark and you'll soon know if a spark can be struck off them. You don't need a big piece of stone; a lump the size of a small walnut will last for months.

The best thing to use for the steel is a small piece of an old file; it must be hard and it must be one of the carbon steels such as is used for the blades of knives, bayonets, and so on. Some alloys, particularly the tungsten types (such as in hacksaw blades) are useless; so is soft iron. If you can't get a bit of an old file the charger from a clip of cartridges will do. Heat it to a clear red in a fire, then dip about one-eighth of an inch of the edges in cold water and hold them there until the steel ceases to hiss.

The only substitute which you can pick up in the bush is iron pyrites; this is the hard and brassy-looking iron ore which is so often mistaken for gold by amateur prospectors.

When you want to use the outfit, open the tinder tin and place it on the ground in a spot sheltered from rain and wind. Hold the bit of rock in your left hand about six inches above the tinder, take the piece of steel in your right hand, and strike a *light*, swift and glancing blow with a sharp edge of the steel across a sharp corner of the rock. A shower of sparks should follow. With a little practice you will find it easy to hold the flint and steel and strike your blow so that the sparks fall on the tinder. Where each spark falls, a glowing spot will appear on the tinder; pick out one of these smouldering pieces, place it on some paper, dry rubbed bark, or dry kangaroo, horse or cow manure, and blow gently until you get a flame. Tinder alone will never give a flame.

Always clap the lid on your tinder tin the moment you have picked out a smouldering piece of timber; if it is left open, tinder rapidly burns to ash.

So simple is the acquiring of the knack of using flint and steel and so light and handy is the outfit, that many soldiers, in places where matches are hard to get or are liable to become useless through damp, now use it in preference to matches.

Failing flint and steel, the next best method is the bow drill. For this you need a piece of thin, flexible stick about two feet long, a piece of thin cord some six inches longer than the stick, and the firestick and drill.

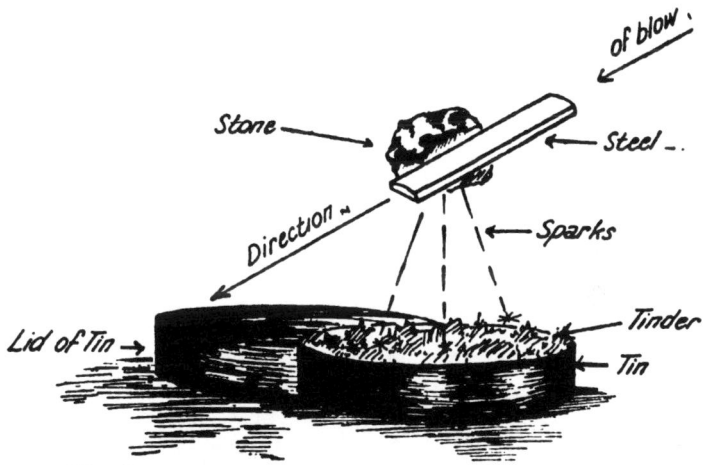

Fig. 1. FLINT AND STEEL , STRIKING SPARK INTO TINDER BOX .

Everything depends upon the last two. They must be the right kind of wood and must be dry; your selection is a very narrow one, because only certain species of plants grow the right sort of wood. Best of all for your drill is the flower stalk of the blackboy (or yacca) tree, next comes lantana, messmate, cottonwood, brown kurrajong. If you have to experiment, use woods of a soft, straight grain which will grind to powder; don't waste time on woods which merely get hot at the point and make a smell of burning without producing powder. Short of being brittle, the older the wood the better. The drill should be about 9 in. long by ¾ in. diameter, quite straight and round, and pointed at either end,

For the firestick you should select a piece of a thick, hard, dry old blackboy flower stalk, or a slab of "snap and rattle" mallee wood, or wild peach, or bone-dry driftwood (other than pine), or the best stuff available. The firestick should be flat on both sides and about three-quarters of an inch thick. In the middle of one edge cut a notch about three-quarters of an inch wide and half an inch deep. wider on the underside so that the powder from the drill falls clear on to the tinder below without jamming in the notch.

9

Just at the back of the notch make a little hole for the point of the drill to turn in. The top bearing of the drill is another but smaller bit of wood with a hollow in the centre to act as the top bearing for the drill.

You oil this top bearing with grease, soap, lead pencil scrapings or even by rubbing it on the side of your nose or through your hair. On no account lubricate the bottom bearing. If your drill doesn't grind itself away properly, put a pinch of sand into the hole and try again.

To use the drill you lay the firestick on the ground and hold it down firmly with your left foot. Take one turn around the drill stick with the cord of the bow, put the bottom point of the drill into the pit beside the notch, place your left arm around the outside of your left leg, wrist held steady by pressing against the ankle, and place the top bearing on the upper end of the drill. Grip the end of the bow in your right hand. Now move the bow to and fro, keeping both stick and string parallel to the ground. The drill stick will spin as the cord turns it. Don't hurry and don't try to get a fire right away —that's an example of learning the hard way. You should start off very slowly and not attempt to get a fire until you have mastered the whole technique of the business — steady movement of bow, top bearing held perfectly steady in the left hand, firestick held down firmly with the left foot, and drill stick spinning without jumping out of the bearings or wobbling.

Lift out the drill stick when you are sure you can use the bow properly, and have a look at the bottom bearing. It should now be worn down until it is a smooth, half-round hole with the notch reaching almost to its centre. Place your tinder— dry and fibrous bark rubbed to fluff, old and dry kangaroo or horse manure, or rubbed and shredded grass or teased cotton— directly under the notch in the firestick with no loose ends sticking up to catch in the drill, and make an attempt to get a fire. Start moving the bow slowly at first, put a very light but steady pressure on the top bearing, and gradually increase both speed and pressure when you see smoke rising from the drill point.

Now comes the thing which many beginners find somewhat bewildering. The spark isn't something which reveals itself by glowing redly; it is quite black. At first only a dry, brown powder is ground away by the drill point, to fall through the notch and on to the tinder below, but as the smoke from the drill point thickens and becomes more pungent in smell, the powder becomes darker in colour and tends more and more to stick together. Finally it collects into a black lump in the notch, from which a faint thread of smoke still arises when you stop drilling and lay the outfit aside. Pick up the tinder

with that black lump in the centre and breathe on it very
gently. A red glow appears in the centre of the lump, spreads
rapidly, and in a couple of seconds you have a big, hot spark,
about the size of the glowing tip of a cigarette. Keep blowing
gently on it until the surrounding tinder is also glowing, then
blow hard and it will burst into flame.

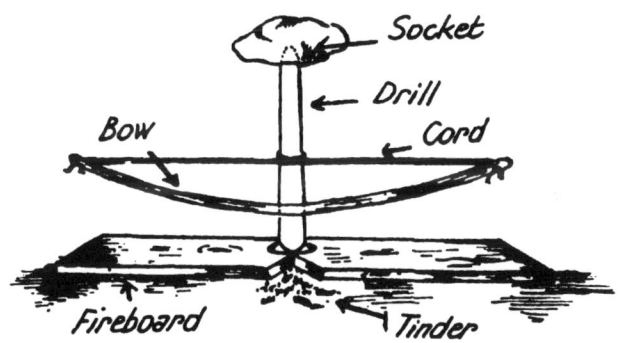

Fig. 2. FIREMAKING WITH BOW AND DRILL

It takes the average student about an hour to pick up the
knack of using the bow drill correctly, and the spare time of
a week or so to master the trick fully. It is also very important
to make sure that you always have a bit of stout cord with
you; at the first opportunity replace your identity disc string
with a piece of strong fishing line or pull-through lanyard.
Then, should — say — a ship be torpedoed and you are forced
to swim ashore, to land naked upon a sea beach, you should still
be able to get a fire going by using sharp-edged sea shells for
a knife and that cord for the bowstring.

Getting the first fire going is always the most difficult
thing; once one fire has been lit you can dry out tinder and
make the lighting of later fires much easier. You can use
sound leather bootlaces to make the cord for the bow, but
when using leather always damp it first, twist it up fairly
tightly, and allow to dry out before using. If you don't do
this, leather will chafe through very rapidly.

You can make a fire without a bow; you use a smooth and
perfectly straight stick about half an inch in diameter and two
feet long for the drill. You twirl this between the palms of

11

your hands; as your hands slip down the drill, you make a
swift snatch at the top of the stick and start twirling it again
without the loss of a second. If there are two of you the
work can be made much easier by the other one holding a top
bearing on the point of the stick.

Fire-lighting by friction is very easy on a blazing hot day
and very difficult on a cold, damp one; the man who can
light a fire by twirling a stick between the palms of his hands
when everything is cold and damp has accomplished a feat
which only one person in a 100 can do — and that only after
a lot of practice.

Chapter Two

GETTING WATER

YOU cannot do better than to copy the methods used by our own aborigines who knew every trick for getting water where another person would soon die of thirst. It is a tragic fact that most of the people who have died of thirst in Australia have done so with water all around them; they didn't realise it was there, or didn't know how, when and where to get it. In a true desert, of course, you will find no water for the simple reason there is none to find. But water can often be found in the most barren-looking country — if you know what to do.

We will start with scrub country where the aborigines could often get water at a pinch from the roots of trees. You mustn't run away with the idea that the root of any tree or plant which you find growing in Australia will yield water; the range of plants and trees which yield water from the root is a limited one, but fortunately you'll find one or another of the right species practically anywhere in our scrub or forest country, from the bottom end of Western Australia to the tip of Cape York. Here's a list of the best water-yielding trees of Australia, so far as getting it from the roots is concerned:—

Western Australia.—Water mallee, blue mallee, York gum, marri, coast wattle, wire-leaf mulga, goldfields water tree, kurrajong, banksias (practically all species) and calathamnos bush.

South Australia.—Water mallee, boobialla, needle bush, pink gum, some species of wattles, nearly all species of banksia.

Victoria.—Nearly all species of banksia, grey box, yellow box, boobialla, many of the wattles.

N.S.W.—Many of the banksias and wattles, ironbark, many of the gum trees with a white, smooth bark, some of the stringybarks.

Queensland.—Many of the wattles, some of the gum trees with smooth bark, most of the banksias.

How to get Water from Roots

Do not go into thick scrub; always, if possible, pick a tree or bush which stands out on its own, grows on the edge of a clearing or on the outer edge of a clump. The bigger, healthier and greener your tree looks, the better your chances of getting plenty of water. You will get most water at sunrise, least in the middle of a hot afternoon. It is often better to choose a tree growing up on a sand ridge rather than one growing in a hollow. Water roots run just under the surface and are straight, have a smoother bark than other roots, and do not have a lot of offshoots growing off them. They may fork into two or three, but generally you can get from 10 to 20 feet of root in one piece, measuring from half an inch in diameter under the bark in some species to two to three inches in others. Cut these roots into two foot lengths, put the end of each *which was nearest to the tree* downward, and let the water drain out. Each length yields from a teaspoon to a quarter of a pint or more, according to the species of tree and the size of the root. If the water does not run out readily, blow down the root. If that fails, get some good clay, moisten a small quantity to make a paste like putty, smear it on the end of the root which was farthest from the tree, prop these sealed ends up on a bank of sand or a large stone, put the other ends into a mess tin or something else which will catch the water, and light a small fire under the row of roots. The heat of the fire generates steam pressure inside the roots; the steam cannot escape through the clay and drives all the moisture out of the other ends of the roots and into the water container. Have you ever noticed moisture bubbling out of the ends of wet sticks when they are placed in a fire?

Always make the cuts on either end of the root as clean as possible, cut on the slant, and it also wise to force the clay well into the pores of the root by pressing with the ball of the thumb, in order to ensure a gastight joint. Before going into bad country you should always get a lump of clay about the size of a walnut and carry it with you. Most water trees grow on a sandhill country — and in that type of country clay is very, very hard to find. Carrying that little lump of clay, wrapped in a bit of old groundsheet and stowed in a corner of basic pouch or haversack, is simply one of those— apparently — trifling things which distinguish the real bush-man from the man whose lack of forethought lands himself— and often his mates as well — into trouble.

Trees Which Yield Water from the Trunk

Many trees which will not yield water from their roots will do so from the trunk. Without exception these are either gum trees or tea trees. Choose a young and healthy sapling about four inches in diameter under the bark at the butt end and 12 to 20 feet long. Cut it off close to the ground and cut off the leafy head, turn it upside down and let the water run out. Whether in selecting a tree to yield water from the trunk or the roots the same rules apply — its green and healthy appearance, time of day to do the job, and so on. If the water won't run out, leave the sapling upside down for a quarter of an hour, cut off the lowest portion, from 18 inches to 2 feet in length, and blow down it as you did with the root. This trick often works with limbs cut from large trees. From an apparently waterless piece of wood you can blow as much as a teacup of water at times.

IMPORTANT.—Never drink water from roots or tree trunks if it has a bitter or sharp taste. Never attempt to drink the liquid which runs out of anything which has a milky juice. Generally speaking, the water should be clean, clear and almost tasteless.

The chief water-yielders from the trunks are:—

Western Australia.—Jarrah, karri, wandoo, flooded gum.

South Australia.—Stringybark, grey box, red gum, manna gum.

Victoria.—Grey box, stringybark, red gum, manna gum, and many other forest trees.

N.S.W.—Same as in Victoria, plus the ironbark.

Queensland.—Ironbark, Queensland bluegum, sugar gum, many other gum trees and tea trees, though the water in the lastnamed is sometimes salty.

It is important to practice getting water from trees because after a time the student becomes so experienced that he can tell a water tree at a glance and, if transferred to another area, can discover which are water trees there by making a few experiments.

Never attempt to use roots or tree trunks in jungle country. Instead, use water vines, which have a rough bark and are a clear cream or pinkish colour inside, with a small brown spot in the centre. Cut up and drain as you would with water roots but never blown down or suck at vines, as this will give you a very sore mouth. Other good water yielders are the lawyer cane (rattan) and the supplejack cane (which resembles a lawyer cane in the stem but grows singly instead of in clumps and hasn't the hooked spines of the lawyer cane).

Identification of Timber

It is as easy to distinguish one tree from another — and to remember it afterwards — as it is to recognise one man from another. You merely note carefully the character of the bark (smooth, rough, grey, white, and so on), the colour of the heartwood (white, yellow, brown, red, and so on), shape and colour of leaves, shape and size of the seed pods, colour of the flowers, any other distinguishing features, the area in which it grows, and you should know that tree if you ever see it again. You don't have to remember *all* trees — merely those which are useful to you. It may seem puzzling at first to the beginner, but with the aid of a notebook to refresh your memory you will soon learn, and it then becomes as easy to tell a messmate from a bluegum as it is to tell a cabbage from a turnip or a petunia from a carnation.

Water from Frogs

This trick has saved the lives of thousands of aborigines and whites alike. When good rain falls on the inland country, and when the wet season arrives in the monsoonal rain country across the upper portion of Australia, all the creek channels, lagoons and swamps fill with water. Within a few hours they are alive with frogs — which did not fall from the sky. They emerged from the mud. When that waterhole dried up, months or even years before, all the frogs filled themselves with water and burrowed into the mud, making neat little cells in the upper layer of the clay, and so they could lie dormant until the next rain arrived to set them free.

But don't think that you can walk out on to the mud of a dry swamp, dig up any amount of frogs anywhere and proceed to get large quantities of water with ease. It's a bit more complicated than that. You must first choose the right type of waterhole — one on which the dry mud has caked and cracked until it resembles a crazy pavement. It is no use choosing a shallow claypan in which water would not lie long enough to give tadpoles a chance to mature into frogs; it must be deep enough to hold water for several weeks. Having located a waterhole of the right type, remember that the frogs don't wait for the swamp to dry before they dig in; they do it when there is still a fair amount of water left.

Find the lowest point in the dry waterhole and ask yourself, "Where was the margin of the last big pool when it was still about 18 inches to two feet deep in the middle?" That is easy enough to see; it is on or near that ring around the lowest point that most of the frogs burrowed in. You may have to dig nine inches to find them and you may have to go nearly two feet; it all depends on the distance at which the clay lies. You will find the frogs, distended with water, in their little mud cells. Pick each one out, hold it mouth downward, and when you squeeze it gently it will disgorge the water. If any man thinks he would sooner go waterless than drink the liquid which has been stored in a frog's guts for a year or so, he immediately reveals the fact that he has never been *really* thirsty.

Collecting Dew

Here is the most valuable tip of the lot; it may save your life when everything else lets you down. Always carry with you a bit of clean sponge about the size of an egg. With its aid, at the first streak of dawn, when the dew lies thickest, you can gather dew from leaves, grass and stones; you can also gather the drops left hanging on the leaves after a light shower of rain. When the sponge becomes sodden, squeeze it into your water container, and hurry — in dry areas that dew will vanish in a few minutes when the dawn wind springs up or the first beams of the sun strike it. The aborigines gathered water by using a pad of dry, fibrous grass which had been chewed and fluffed until it resembled cotton wool; a sponge, of course, is far more efficient. You need a lot of practice to become proficient at dew collecting — and once again you have the alternative of two ways of learning how to do it, the easy way being to get in that practice now and the hard way being to wait for the actual emergency to arise.

If you haven't a sponge, use cotton wool, a pad made of towelling, or some woollen rag.

Moisture from Leaves

Two plants which will give you a drink, of a sort, are the "pig-face" weed of the coastal areas, and the parakylia of the inland sandhills. Both have thick, fleshy leaves; crush them to extract the juice, boil it if possible. Never gather pig-face leaves in a salt swamp; they are too salty to use. Get them off sandhills or where they grow in chinks in the rocks.

Bird Guides to Water

Some of our native birds are infallible guides to water, particularly wild pigeons, which always go to drink at sunset in warm weather. In very hot weather they also drink at dawn. There are five main species of pigeon: the bronzewing,

17

widely distributed in Australia and found in the scrub and forest country of W.A., S.A., Victoria, N.S.W. and Central Australia; the topknot or wirewing, found mostly in forest country; the squatter, a bird of the open plains; the flock pigeon, found on the plains of inland Queensland; and the rock pigeon, found in very rocky, broken country or among craggy hills. The flight of a wild pigeon is quite distinctive and a trained eye can tell it from that of any other bird at any distance up to 300-400 yards with ease.

The easy way to learn how to use the wild pigeon as a guide is to go to a waterhole whose position you know and to sit down near the bank towards sunset, keeping quite still. Your first lesson is merely to sit there and watch the pigeons come in to drink. Next evening, go back some 300 yards from the waterhole and watch the pigeons flying past as they make for the waterhole, noting how all the lines of flight converge on the one spot, indicating the position of the water.

On the following evening take up your position some 600 yards from the waterhole and again watch those lines of flight, and keep on, evening after evening, until you are at least three miles back from the water, where you may see no more than one or two pigeons. By that time your eye should be trained to pick up the flight of a pigeon and see the direction in which it is heading; then you can go out in an entirely different direction, watch for pigeons on the wing, and locate another waterhole solely by the direction indicated by the pigeons' lines of flight.

How do you tell if a bird is flying in to drink or is heading for home? When you've had a lot of experience you'll be able to do that at a glance, but the beginner had better rely on the fact that birds going to drink are all converging on the one spot, while those which have had a drink are heading in different directions.

Don't try to hurry that part of your training; never was there a better illustration of the truth of the old Chinese proverb, "Walkee softly, catchee monkey."

Birds which tell you that water is near at hand (although they don't actually guide you to it) are the zebra finches or waxbills; the cock bird has striped feathers on its breast and a beak the colour of red sealing wax. Usually you don't locate these birds by sight; the first indication of their presence is their "tsip-tsip" cry, very similar to the snipping of a pair of scissors. The chestnut-eared finch is another guide; it is a small grey bird with a tan-coloured patch of feathers on either cheek, and can be identified by its cry of "teut-teut, teut-teut" which has a note like a child's tin trumpet. Bushmen call it the "headache bird" on account of its monotonous cry. No matter how dry the country may look, if you find that either of those birds are present you can say to yourself for certain there is water within a mile or so of me. If it weren't the birds wouldn't be there.

In forest country the same thing holds good if you hear the clear, melodious "wardle-warp" call of the river dove, or the "pee-wee" of the mudlark. Any swallows which build a mud nest like that of the mudlark — the cliff marten or "bottle-nest" swallow is one — are also never found far from water, but never let yourself be fooled by the presence of a kingfisher. It can, and often does, live far from water, in spite of the popular idea that it lives only on creek banks and fishes for a living. Nobody can learn how to use birds as a water guide by reading instructions; you can learn how to do it, and how to identify your birds, only by actual practice, as advised in case of pigeons.

Aboriginal Camp Sites

Our aborigines seldom camped far from the water, because it had to be carried to the camp, and they never camped right alongside it, as so many white people do, because that would scare away game coming in to drink. From 200-400 yards is the usual distance. It follows, therefore, that any sign of an aboriginal camp is a fairly reliable guide to a water supply being nearby. The water supply might have been a seasonal one, which existed only in a good season or after a heavy rain; this possibility should always be taken into account.

In searching for an aboriginal camp site, bear in mind these facts. They never camped on a flat if there were a rise handy, even if it were only a few feet above the surrounding ground; they liked shelter from the prevailing winds, and they needed a firewood supply. They preferred soft or sandy ground to rocks and pebbles.

Along the coasts it is usually easy to pick out their old camp sites by the mounds of shells mixed with ashes and calcined bones; in other places you'll find heaps of fire-blackened rocks which had formed the base of their cooking ovens. Further guides are worn and bruised stones which had been used as hammers; flat stones worn into a hollow on the face which have been used to grind grass seeds into flour; and small chips of flint, chert, quartz, bottle-glass or the porcelain from telegraph insulators which had been used for knives and scrapers. Often these discarded implements will be found scattered over an area of ground as much as an acre in extent. Having located the camp site, and if the water supply is not an obvious one, such as a soak, spring or rockhole, look for spots where vegetation is a guide to the presence of fresh water close to the surface.

Digging for Water

We are not concerned with artesian or sub-artesian water supplies, but with the "ground" water which can be reached at shallow depth with the aid of the tools carried by every Army vehicle or water which, in some cases, can be reached by digging with a bayonet, a pointed stick or even by grubbing with your bare hands. The three main spots where such water can be found are:—

> Around coastal sand dunes or the sandhills around the shores of inland salt lakes.
>
> Sandy creek beds.
>
> In country where there are big, dome-shaped outcrops of impervious rock such as granite.

Always, if possible, choose a spot at the base of a big, wind-blown sandhill that is bare of vegetation; if a sandhill is covered with scrub, the roots of the vegetation are liable to use up the available water. With a windblown sandhill there is also no run-off for the rain; every drop soaks straight in. further, there is no capillary attraction in sand; in clays, loams and soils this brings water to the surface where the sun and the wind dry it out, but any water which soaks into driftsand stays there. Your sandhill is — strange as the idea might seem at first — a water-catcher and, what is more important still, a water holder, if the conditions are favourable. Much of the rain which soaks into sand is lost because it goes on down into the lower layers of the sub-soil, although here and there a sheet of impervious rock, or a bed of clay, will prevent its going any deeper and will form a bed of water-logged sand immediately above the rock or clay, which can be tapped by a well or bore. This is, however, quite rare; what usually happens is that the fresh water comes to rest on top of the layer of salt water which has soaked through from the sea or the salt lake. Another thing, which also seems queer at first, is that a layer of fresh water will float on top of the salt water without mixing, like cream on a pan of milk. When you sink a well in a sandhill, always bear in mind the fact that this fresh water layer may be very thin and that the two layers may become mixed if the balance between them is upset by sinking the well too deep or by drawing on it too heavily.

This problem can be overcome in a very simple way. Get an old bucket, a drum with the top cut out, army biscuit tin, cask with the head knocked out, box with the joints caulked, or even a section of hollow log with the bottom end plugged up with clay. Sink this in the centre of your well so that its upper edge, which must be level, is just an inch below the surface of the water. Then pack the sand back again to within four inches of the surface of the water or, better still, if you can do it, replace it with clay well rammed down. If the sand keeps coming into the hole, drive some stakes and dig inside them.

The sump finished, clear the salt water out of it by taking a tin, turn it upside down, push it slowly to the bottom, let the air bubble out gently, bring it up slowly again, and tip it into a bucket; when the bucket is full, empty it at some distance from the well. Continue the bailing until the water in the sump is quite fresh; the well is then ready for use, and only fresh water will be able to enter your drum. The stunt works because the only water which can enter your drum has to flow from out of the surface layer, where the water is fresh; the salt water lower down cannot get in because the drum is in the road.

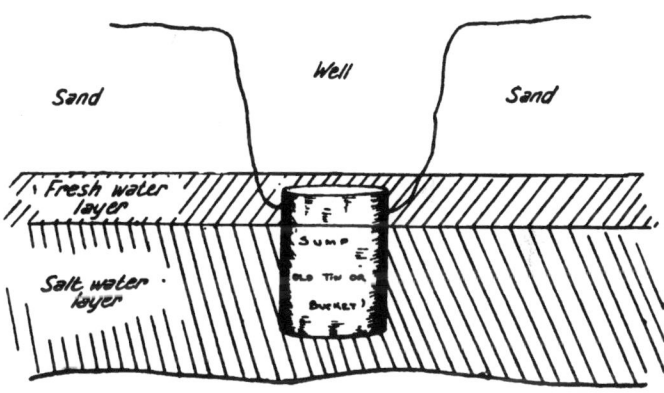

Fig. 3. SUMP TO SHUT OFF SALT WATER

In sandy creek beds you should go along the watercourse looking at the timber on the banks. Where the trees — red gums, flooded gums, box trees, coolibahs, and so on, look very fresh and green (especially if there is a sheoak or two among them), sink a hole in the bed close to the bank. Failing trees, look for spots where wild dogs, kangaroos and horses have been digging for water in the sand.

In looking for water around the big granite outcrops, bear in mind the fact that those impervious rocks shed rainwater just as an iron roof does; most of this water soaks into the soil and is lost. Here and there, however, there are underground beds of sand, gravel or porous rock ("aquifers") which will hold and store this water. You don't have to sink a lot of shafts or cut along trenches across country to locate these beds; you do nothing more than look at the timber. You can be sure of water where you see a vigorous growth of the Geraldton manna gum (really a wattle), or of the swish-bush (a fairly tall, wiry shrub whose twigs spring back with a swishing sound as you push your way through it), or of cork-wood trees (whose bark is something like cork in appearance and whose timber is also very corky in grain; an axe tends to stick in the cut instead of cutting out chips) or of sheoaks, growing close to a big boss of granite. You can sink a well among that timber patch with the assurance that your chances of striking fresh water close to the surface are about 100 to 1.

Here is an idea for getting water from sand which is worth imitating; it is used by our aborigines and also by the Bushmen of South Africa. Instead of sinking shafts to get water from sand, which means a lot of work with sometimes a very real danger of the sand collapsing on the digger, the aborigines and the bushmen of South Africa make a hole in the sand with a long, straight stick, such as the shaft of a spear. They carry a long reed whose joints have been knocked out and with a bunch of grass tied on one end to act as a filter and keep back the sand. When the spear shaft reaches the water, it is withdrawn and the reed is inserted in its place, with the bunch of grass at the bottom and the water sucked up. The spear pump used by the Light Horse in Palestine during the last war was a modern adaption of this device.

Turning a Tree into a Water Catcher

When a shower of rain is approaching and you need some water but have no ordinary means of catching the rain — the usual plan is to tie a groundsheet to stakes or saplings at the four corners and to put a stone in the middle as a weight — you should go to the nearest smooth-barked tree which has a fairly tall and straight trunk. Cut a couple of grooves with your knife in the bark, like those used in tapping rubber trees, starting on the side from which you expect the rain to come, and giving them a sharp and uniform fall towards the leeward side of the tree, where they will meet at an angle like a letter V. At the bottom of the V stick a gumleaf or piece of bark into the bark to act as a spout. The upper side of the groove should be about an inch high and the bottom one should be about one quarter of an inch deep and should slant inwards. You have, in effect, a gutter around the tree. When the squall of rain strikes the tree the water runs down the bark and into the groove; then it runs around and down the groove to the spout, under which you can hold a water-bottle or bucket to catch it.

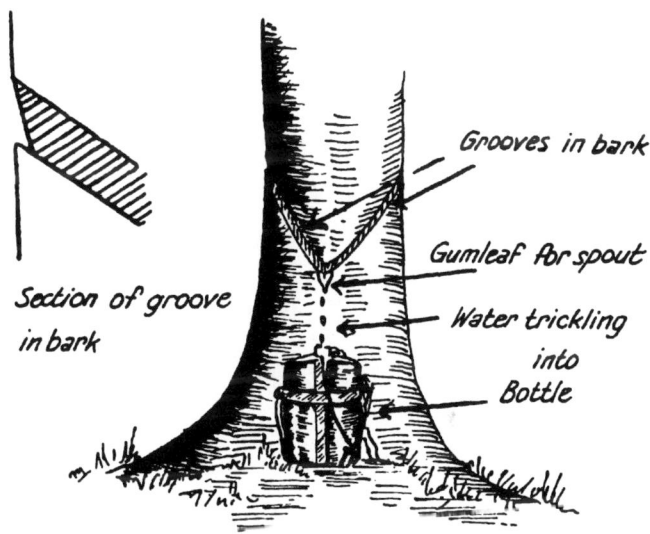

Grooves in bark

Gumleaf for spout

Water trickling
into
Bottle

Section of groove
in bark

Fig 4. TREE AS WATER CATCHER

Chapter Three

DEVELOPING AN EYE FOR COUNTRY

YOU want to discover something such as scrub in which food or water can be found, or to pick out the spots where aborigines would camp, provided there was water handy, or to discover the best route to follow. You go to the nearest rise, stand on the top, and let your eye scan the surrounding terrain. There it is, something like a relief map, with everything you want to know plainly marked — the sheltered sides of the sand ridges where aborigines would be likely to camp, the line of timber which indicates the course of a creek, the flat-topped hill with the clump of timber at its base which might indicate the presence of a spring, the patches of acacias in whose trunks you could find a meal of the edible bardie grubs, the broken, rocky ground dotted with prickly coorara bush, among which you know you will find the convolvulus vine of the coolya — a true yam with an edible root the size of a potato — the patch of country which had a fire over it last year, and upon which kangaroos and other game will come miles to feed. It is all there and you can pick out everything at a glance — if you have the trained bushman's eye for country.

To develop this eye you must train yourself in exactly the same way as you did in the case of learning to follow wild pigeons to water. You begin where everything is quite easy and by slow stages work back to where it is very hard. Begin with something like the Geraldton manna gum (it is really a wattle) which, when growing vigorously with a green and healthy appearance among granite outcrops, shows that fresh water lies close to the surface. You need to know that tree, not only when you see it close up, but when it is a mile or two away. Begin by examining it at close range and pick out its distinguishing features — the way in which the leaves hang, the angle at which most of the branches leave the main stem, and so on — and then take another look at it from a distance of 50 feet. Keep moving back at intervals of 50 feet; you will find that at — say — 200 feet, you can no longer distinguish it from other trees by the features which you have noted. You can still pick it out, however, by the colour of its foliage when contrasted with other trees and the shape in which it grows. Continue to move back until this, too, is no longer of use as a guide as far as individual trees go — but you will find that the colour still enables you to identify a clump of those same trees, with the general appearance of the clump as a further guide. Do the same thing with granite outcrops, limestone ridges, sandhills, tea-tree swamps and all other features which you may have to pick out from a distance; don't try to hurry the job. It is a trick which you can practice without trouble by looking out of the back of a moving truck and keeping your eye on the different features as they recede into the distance.

When you begin to feel that you have mastered the art, reverse the process and see how you get on. Look at a patch of country from a distance of about a mile, then move towards it and see if your estimates of the timber, nature of the soil and so on are correct. You'll probably find it a lot easier than it sounds.

A vitally important point is this: there is a corner in your training which you have to turn before you can start handing compliments to yourself; before you turn that corner it is all hard graft and concentration; once it has been turned, the rest becomes easier and easier. You'll know when the time arrives by the fact that you start to notice things instinctively, without first thinking about it. For example, a wild pigeon flies past you; before you have turned the corner in your training you pause to think, "That looked like a pigeon — yes, it is one. Which way is it heading? Over that way — and, by the sun, that is almost due east. There's water out there." After the corner has been passed you turn your head for an instant, without any pause for thought; the movement is as swift and as involuntary as that which a fisherman uses when he feels a bite on his line. Automatically into your mind jumps the fact that there is water to the eastward of you. In the same way there will come a time when you will automatically note all the important features of the country as you pass along, almost without being aware of the fact; yet, should it be necessary to recall some feature later, you will find that it has been stored away.

Chapter Four

FOOD

RIGHT from the outset, put aside all preconceived notions as to what you will, or won't, eat in an emergency. A starving man will eat anything — and so will you, if you ever feel the gnawing hunger and weakness of starvation yourself. Many say, "I'll eat that when I have to and not before." It's a fool's argument if there ever were one. You have the choice of two ways of learning these things — the easy and the hard; the man who learns *now* how to live off the bush scores heavily if he ever has to do it in earnest; the man who leaves it until the emergency arises has chosen the hard way, and he will be lucky if he lives to tell the story.

We'll presume that you are one of those who refuse to try out the edible bardie (wood) grub as food, preferring to leave it "until you have to." That day arrives, and after some 36 hours without food you say to yourself, "I'd even eat bardie grubs now." All right, you are quite willing to do so — but do you know how to get them *now*? The chances are 10 to 1 that you don't know the first thing about it; as the old adage has it, you first catch the hare before you decide how to cook it.

Some of the native foods which sound least attractive— bardie grubs, snakes, goanna tail — are the best when you have overcome your instinctive distaste. Further, the only way in which you can make sure of being able to find such foods when there is nothing else to eat is to start now on the job of finding and using them. There is no substitute for actual practice in this matter; to do otherwise is just as absurd as it would be to say that you will "Fire your rifle when you have to and not before," on the ground that the recoil will make your shoulder ache if you start practising now.

The bardie grub, also known as the pelattie, witchettie and purdie, has a high place among native foods because it is so easy to secure, because it is so common, and because it is not only a real delicacy, but also an almost perfect food in itself. Eaten raw, it has a flavour something like that of a walnut; cooked in the ashes, it is like scrambled egg.

In yacca country, find a yacca which has been dead about two months and kick it to pieces; you will find the still partly-green heart riddled with the grubs. In wattles, look for heaps of stuff like brown sawdust around the base of the trunk, run your eye up the trunk to locate the grub-hole from which the sawdust is being ejected, and cut out the grub. In mulga and jamwood country you do the same thing; with the coast wattle you go to small, stunted and sickly-looking bushes and try to pull them up by the roots. If they come up easily it is usually because the bardies have eaten out the roots. With trees like the native poplar you select those which have died quite recently and push against them; if they snap off below the ground the cause will usually be that the grubs have eaten out the roots. In big timber country, go to spots which are inclined to be damp in winter, rake away the leaves under a big, old tree, looking for holes in the ground about the size of your thumb. These show that the big root below has been riddled by grubs; you can dig up the root or you can prise out the grubs with either a wire or a thin, pliant twig with a hook on the end; push it down the hole until the grub is reached; the movement of the grub makes itself felt through the twig or wire, and it can be hooked and withdrawn.

Grubs can also be found in the jungle under the sapwood of trees which have been blown down some two or three months previously, or limbs which have fallen. The time when the bark is starting to leave the fallen timber is the right time.

In sago palms, look for those which have died recently. In other trees you look for bulges on the limbs. The man who puts in a bit of practice at grub-hunting soon picks up the knack of locating them, and even if you don't need to eat them yourself they need not be wasted; they are good bait for fish.

Snake

Snake looks like a cross between eel and fish when it has been baked in hot ashes, but the flavour is more like that of roast poultry. Getting a snake when you want it is something of an art; you have to keep your eyes open for recent snake tracks on sand patches, and you have to know just where they may be found — the brown snake handy to hollow logs or rock outcrops which provide hiding places, the black snake in hollows around swamps and creeks, the tiger in similar spots, the carpet snake in patches of timber, and so on. Snake was one of the favourite dishes of the aborigine, and anyone who samples it will agree with the aboriginal taste in that respect, if in no other. The best way to start anyone off on snake as an article of diet is to let him eat some under the impression that it is fish, and tell him what it was afterwards.

Snaring Game

There are many forms of snare and they can be made of stranded brass wire, soft copper or steel wire, string, the long sinews taken from a kangaroo tail, or the intestines of animals which have been cleaned out, twisted, and allow to dry, making a cord of catgut strong enough to hold anything. Plaited horsehair will also serve.

Small split sticks to hold loop steady.

End of snare tied to peg.

Fig 5. SIMPLE SNARE, SET OVER RABBIT RUNWAY OR KANGAROO PAD.

In its simplest form the snare is merely a loop suspended over a game pad with the free end tied to a peg or springy sapling; in its elaborate form it is fastened to the end of a long, springy sapling which is bent down and fastened with a stick trigger and the snare loop is laid flat on the ground.

When the animal knocks the stick trigger, which projects over the pad, it releases the sapling, which whips upward, and the loop catches one of the animal's legs, holding it helpless, with its hind-quarters in the air; or, in the case of a big kangaroo, with one leg in the air, which has almost the same effect.

A word of warning is necessary, however, about these "spring-up" snares. Always do the work of setting the trigger with

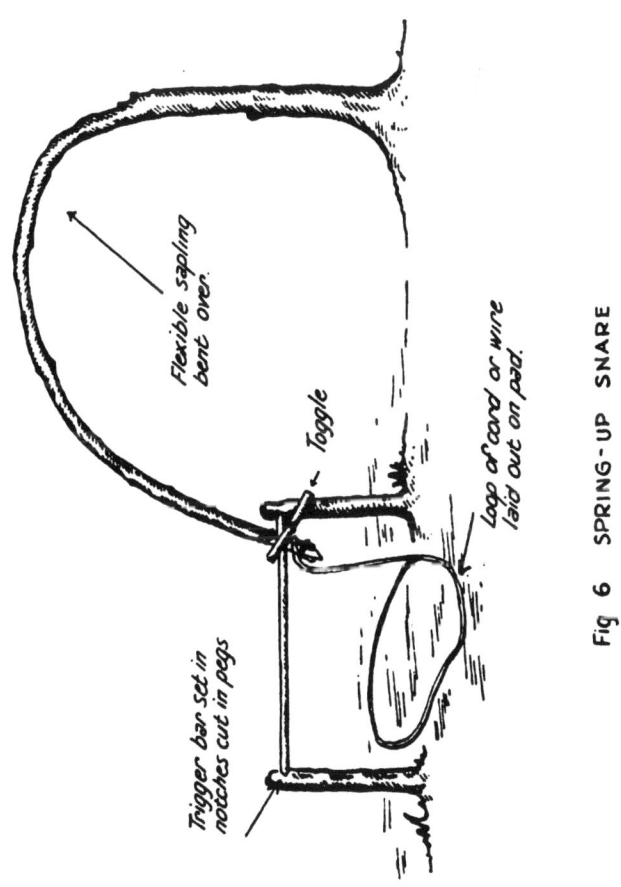

Fig 6   SPRING-UP SNARE

your left arm and shoulder over the bent-down sapling, and keep it there until your head is out of danger when you think it has been set properly. Failure to adopt that precaution has cost many a man some of his front teeth or has given him a broken nose or a black eye. A properly set snare is a very deadly thing and the man who knows how to use one can get game without scaring other animals and without firing shots which will give away his position.

Fish

There is no place in this booklet for the use of dynamite or other explosives as a means of securing fish. Explosives are wasteful, dangerous, and foolish; this is especially true of the use of explosives in inland rivers and creek pools, where they kill everything down to the smallest minnow. Their use means that one man or one party gets a feed of fish, and then everyone else goes without afterwards until that pool becomes stocked again, which may take years to do. You can get just as good results in pools and creeks by stirring up the mud, either with long sticks used from the bank or by wading in and kicking it up with your feet. The mud drives all the fish to the surface; you pick out what you want and leave the rest. As soon as the water clears they go down again, and are left to keep the pool stocked. In small pools fish can often be stunned by smacking together a couple of hard, round stones under water.

Troops on active service seldom have time to spare for fishing in orthodox ways. String nets soon rot and become useless if not cared for properly. The best things are the fish trap and the spear — they give the best and quickest results in competent hands.

Fish Traps

There are several types of fish trap, but the main factor governing success is the choice of site. For the "maze" type of trap the best site is the mouth of a tidal creek or inlet, into which fish travel with the tide at night to feed in the shallows, returning again to the sea on the ebb. Across the mouth of the inlet you should build walls of loose stones, fences of stakes spaced like pickets, or lay down lines of thick brushwood kept in place by stakes. Fish entering the inlet have no trouble in making their way upstream, but when they try to leave again on the falling tide they become trapped in the angles of the fences. The water drains out through the chinks in the stones or the interstices of the sticks, and undersized fish escape this way. Traps of this type should always be visited at dawn if the tide has ebbed during the night, otherwise the trapped fish may provide a feed for the pelicans and gulls. Where the tide runs strongly, weeds and other rubbish are liable to pile against the walls, damming back the water and causing such pressure that only a well-built structure can withstand the strain; it is often easier in the long run to put your trap at a spot where the channel is fairly wide and the current slow, even if it means more building of fences.

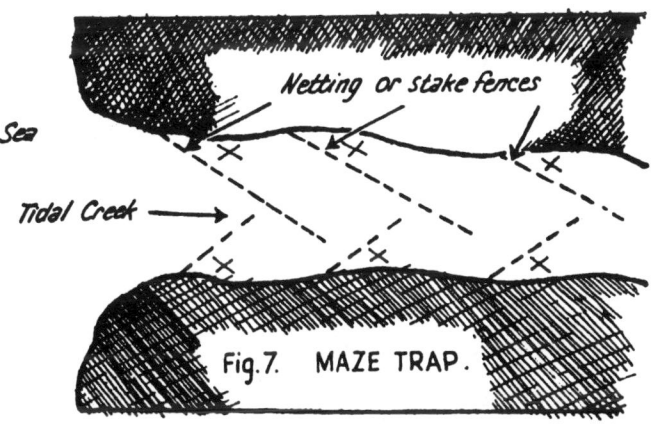

Fig. 7. MAZE TRAP.

With this type of trap, always probe the mud or sand in the angles of the fences with a stick; many fish, such as the flounder, bury themselves except for their mouth and eyes when they find themselves trapped in shallow water.

Far easier to make and to use is the drumnet, although it doesn't make the big catches of the maze trap. It is best made of wire netting, but if this not available, you can use canes, jungle vines, lignum shoots or pliant green sticks. You should make the drumnet's framework from sticks and hoops, with a funnel-like opening at each end; this frame is covered with wire netting or a mesh of canes interwoven like a very open-weaved basket. If the sticks you use won't bend without breaking, you can make them pliant by burying them under the ashes of a fire for a short time. When using the drumnet in fresh water set it with wings of netting or stakes to guide the fish into the opening; the best spots in rivers are narrow channels connecting two deep pools or across the mouth of a billabong running back from the main stream.

In the sea, always pick a spot sheltered from the waves or heavy currents, and remember this important point: when moving from one feeding ground to another — and most fish come into the shallow, sheltered bays to feed at night — fish always "cut the corner," so make use of this by placing the net at the end of a line of rocks which run out to sea, or on the point of a cape. By doing this, you pick up the fish as they go around the corner, so to speak. No matter where it is set, a drumnet always works best if it is baited with a bit of fresh, raw meat in the centre, or some crushed crabs or crayfish.

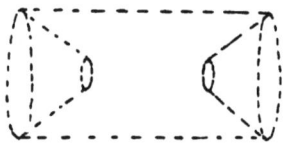

Fig. 8.(A) DRUMNET

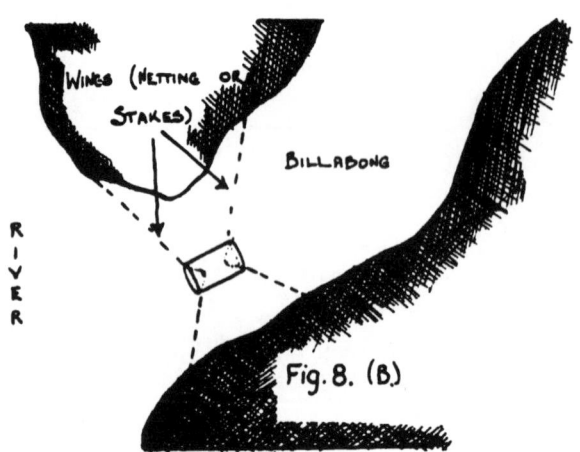

Fig. 8. (B.)

SETTING A DRUMNET IN MOUTH OF BACKWATER

King of all fish traps, however, is the "arrowhead" or "Queensland" type. Pick a site in a sheltered bay because heavy waves will soon knock the whole thing flat, and run the main fence straight out to sea to a spot where there will be some six inches of water at low tide; the fences must be out of water to a height of some 12 inches at high tide. If there is a big rise and fall in your particular locality it does not matter if the trap is high and dry at low tide. The trap can be built of wire netting fastened to stakes, steel mesh or stake fences. The head of the trap need not be very big; the usual size is ten feet across the widest part by about six feet from point to base. The two entrances are just wide enough for a man to walk through, and the gap at the head of the fence is the same size.

This trap works because fish, when they meet an obstruction, always head towards deep water to get around it. Therefore a school of fish, when it strikes the main fence, follows it out to sea. This brings the fish to one of the entrances to the trap; they go in, swim to the head, follow the fence around inside the "arrowhead" and thus come to the main fence again. They head out to sea to get around it once more, and round they go again. They always end up by milling around, hopelessly

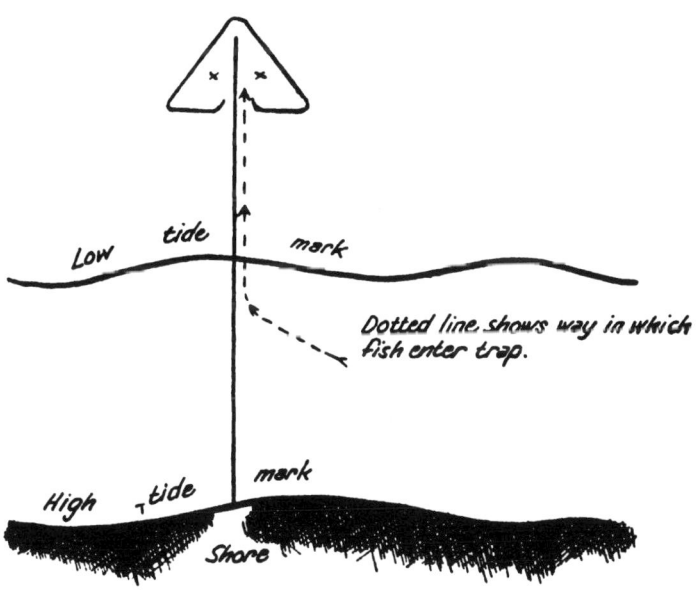

Fig. 9. "ARROWHEAD" TRAP

bamboozled, at the spots marked X on the sketch. When the tide falls they can be speared, scooped up with a dip net or killed by hitting them across the back.

One of these traps in a good position will feed a company of men, day after day.

Fish Spears

Fish spears should be used from a boat or a raft of the cater-maran type. This can be built of light logs placed side by side and fastened by cross-battens nailed or lashed to the logs; failing logs, use bundles of reeds or bamboos. Fish spears are of two types, heavy and light. The former has a shaft made from a strong young sapling and the head is made from stiff wire bent into four prongs, in size and shape like those of a garden fork. You make the barbs by file cuts or by flattening the points and cutting them with a cold chisel. Besides spear and boat or raft, you need a water glass, which should be made of wood with a sheet of glass puttied into the bottom, but you can make do with a half-gallon tin with a hole cut in the bottom, over which a bit of glass has been stuck with bitumen, adhesive tape, or anything else which will make a watertight joint.

You press the bottom end under the surface of the water and look down the tin and through the piece of glass in the bottom; this enables you to scan the sea floor as you drift along, with all the light reflections and the ripples shut off. To use the heavy spear, wait until you see a sizable fish nosing around among the rocks or weeds, pin it down with a thrust of the spear, hold it until its first violent struggles are over, and then haul it aboard.

The light spear is the same as the heavy one, except for its size; the four prongs can be of comparatively light wire, the head need not be more than six inches wide, and a stout bamboo will do for the shaft. At first you'll find it difficult to use, because the light spear is intended for spearing from the bank; you will not be more or less directly over the fish, as you were in the boat or on the raft, but well to one side of it. You must allow for the refraction of the water before trying to spear the fish; it isn't where it seems to be, but is much nearer. When you take aim, strike as if you wanted the spear to pass under the fish on the nearer side. Before trying your hand on fish, it is a good idea to get in some practice by picking bits of weed or other rubbish off the bottom; this will soon teach you how much to allow for refraction in varying depths of water.

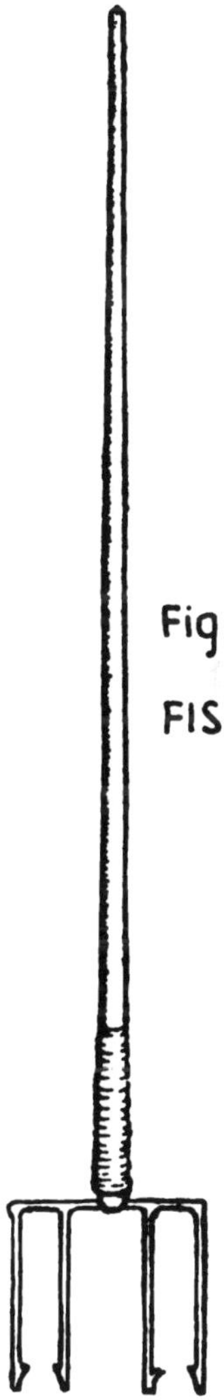

Fig. 10.

FISH SPEAR

The best places to use the light spear are pools among mangroves at low tide, or off the edge of a reef. Always move slowly as you search for fish; even the expert doesn't always see the fish when he first glances into the water, because nature has camouflaged them too well. Look hard at every mangrove root, every rock crevice and every patch of weed; keep your eyes open for what looks like a little bit of loose bark or seaweed waving in a current, or a red streak which appears and disappears with the regularity of a clock ticking. Stare hard at that spot and suddenly the fish will appear; what you took to be a piece of bark is a fin waving, and the disappearing red streak is the gill opening and closing as the fish breathes. When a fish has been sighted, lower your spear slowly to within a foot of it, make the correct allowance for refraction, give a swift thrust, and you'll have him.

Don't turn up your nose at a young shark; it provides very tasty boneless cutlets. A bit of stingray flapper is also good, but you should grill it; don't fry it, because it is too oily that way. If you think you have never tried shark or stingray before you'll probably find you're wrong; both have been on the market for years under fancy names such as "flake," skate," etc.

There are a few poisonous fish in Australian waters; they belong chiefly to the toadfish and boxfish types. The old idea that if a silver coin turns black when placed in contact with the flesh of a poisonous fish is pure hooey. Your best plan is to reject, without question, any fish of the toadfish species, or any other unusual-looking, striped and highly-coloured fish if you don't already know them as being good for food, and not to rely on any old-wives' tales of the silver-coin variety.

There are no poisonous shellfish around the coasts of Australia, and practically all are edible, although some are very tough and rank. The best way to cook most shellfish is to lay them on hot coals until they begin to steam; with very tough kinds it is best to remove from the shell and to beat well with, say, the back of a bayonet on a stone until the meat has been reduced to shreds before cooking. In many of our inland freshwater creeks and lagoons you'll find an edible mussel if you grope in the sand or mud in shallow water close to the shore. This mussel is about the size of a large cockle, and it has a very insipid taste, even when well sprinkled with salt.

Fig. 11.—POISONOUS FISH.

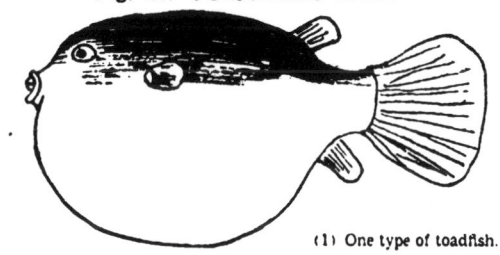

(1) One type of toadfish.

(2) One type of porcupine fish.

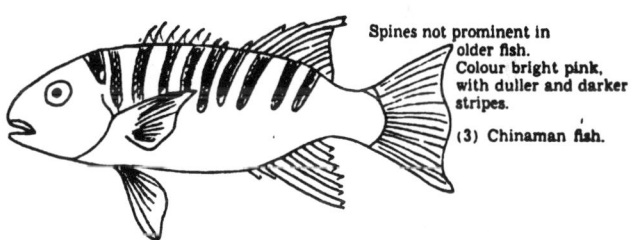

Spines not prominent in older fish.
Colour bright pink, with duller and darker stripes.

(3) Chinaman fish.

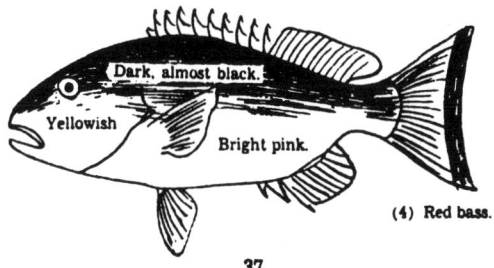

Dark, almost black.

Yellowish

Bright pink.

(4) Red bass.

Vegetables

Edible roots and leaves are rare in some parts of Australia, although even in these there are far more of them than one would imagine. Their nutritive value is not high as a rule, though here again there are exceptions. Spinach can be made from several native and imported plants; among the former is the leaf of the "old-man" saltbush and the creeping plant with a heart-shaped leaf known as "native spinach," while among the latter are the leaves of stinging nettles, milk thistles, lucerne and clovers. The young white leaves, found in the heart of the blackboy, yacca and grass trees of Australia, are tender and have an agreeable nutty flavour.

A surprising number of plants in Australia form edible tubers on the roots; this is especially true of plants of the convolvulus family, and of many of our orchids. These roots, generally known by the all-embracing name of "yam," range in size from a tiny white radish-like thing about an inch in length by a quarter of an inch in diameter, with a watery, raw-potato flavour, to large tubers very like a sweet potato in flavour and food value. You find them in the most unexpected places; under a large green bush, as in the Exmouth Gulf area of Western Australia, or under a single leaf like that of an onion (but yellow in colour), near Perth. They may look like a bunch of grapes and be found under a little plant with a pretty violet flower, in the lower part of South Australia, or grow on the root of a little vine found under fallen timber or in the shelter of prickly bushes in other parts of Australia. Aborigines or experienced bushmen can usually tell you which plants carry edible tubers in any part of the country.

The young sprout of the bullrush, too, makes a vegetable almost as good as asparagus. Many of the waterlilies have an edible bulb, but in some cases these bulbs need special treatment before being cooked and eaten.

There are a few edible nuts to be found in the bush, such as the quandong and the sandalwood nut, and a few fruits and berries, but there are very many which are either inedible or poisonous, and it would take a large book to describe them all and list the places where they are to be found. One thing must be emphasised: the fact that birds can be seen eating a certain seed or berry is NOT a sign that human beings can eat them wtihout ill effects; wild pigeons, for example, can eat the berries of the strychnine bush, but we can't.

Bush Cookery

The art of cooking without utensils is one well worth studying; it needs practice to gain proficiency, but often the results compare favourbly with anything which comes out of the oven.

The chief method is to bake in the ashes. Dig a shallow trench a little bigger than the article to be cooked, light a fire in it, and let it burn down to ash. Do not hurry this part of the job; you have to heat up the surrounding earth or sand for thorough cooking, and that takes time. In some cases you can get a more lasting heat if you line the trench with stones. Brush out the ash and place whatever you have to cook in it; in the case of birds, leave the feathers on; with animals, singe off the fur but do not skin; do not gut or scale fish. Cover with the ash and light a small but steady fire on top.

The time required depends upon the size of the piece to be cooked; a one-pound fish should be done in about twenty minutes, but a large leg of kangaroo may take more than an hour. Like baking of a damper, practice is needed. When you think the meat is cooked, brush away the ash, lift out with a sheet of bark, and you will find that skin, fur or feathers peel off quite easily, taking all adhering ash and sand with them. A variant of this method is to wrap the food in wet paper, or in the soft type of bark found on trees like the paper-bark tea-tree or in banana and paw paw leaves, before burying in the hot ash. Or, you can mix up some clay with water to the consistency of soft dough and then coat the bird, fish, animal or joint with it. Edible roots, eggs, crabs, shellfish and small "johnny cakes" made of edible native seeds which have been crushed between two stones and then moistened with a little water can all be baked in the hot ash.

Chapter Five

MISCELLANEOUS HINTS

BUSHCRAFT does not consist of mastering any one big thing, but of gaining proficiency in many little points. Here are some; a good student will go on adding to them for the rest of his life.

A Drinkable Liquid from Fish

Cut the meat from a freshly-caught fish into small slices. Place in the sleeve of a shirt or any other stout piece of cloth, and twist up tightly, just as you do when wringing out washed clothes. A small quantity of a clear liquid will be forced through the cloth. You can drink it because it is free of salt.

Emergency Water Container

If you have to improvise a water container, copy the Arabs, the Mexican Indians or our aborigines, whose water skins are older than recorded history. Strip the skin, like a sleeve, off any small animal (rabbit, opossum, wallaby, young goat, etc.), and tie the skin of the hind legs together to form a carrying handle. Tie knots in the forelegs and lash up the neck with twine, sinew or a strip of skin. Leave the fur side in, pack with dry sand and hang up to dry. A short length of the large intestine of a big animal — bullock, buffalo, horse, etc.— can be used in the same way.

Catching Birds with Fishhooks

Birds, such as swans, wild ducks and cranes, can be caught with ease. First go around the swamp or lagoon looking for the spots where they are feeding; in daylight you'll see tracks and droppings on nearby sandbanks or mud spits; at night, listen and look across the water into the reflection of moonlight, starlight or against a light background on the farther shore.

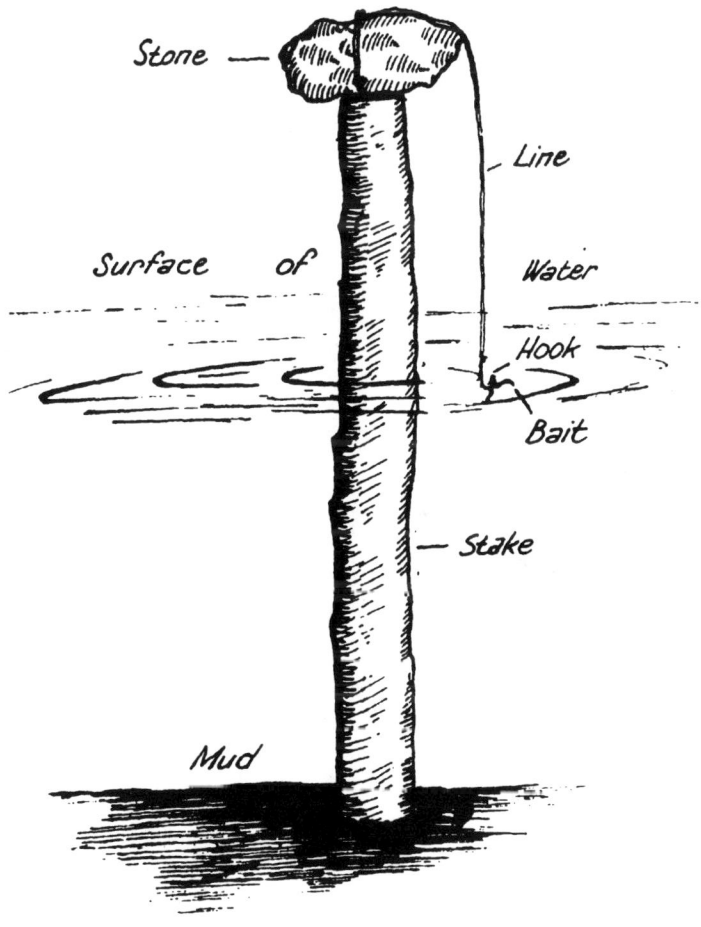

Fig. 12. FISHHOOK SET TO CATCH WILD FOWL

41

Bait your hooks with small brown frogs, centipedes, worms, big
spiders, shellfish meat, grubs, worms or similar stuff. Drive
stakes into the mud where you saw the birds feeding and let
them project about eight inches above the surface. Tie the
line to a stone weighing about four pounds and balance the
stone on the head of the stake; hang the bait so that it just
touches the surface of the water. Always set your baits just
at dusk; if you set your baits in the daytime you may catch
only near-useless birds, such as shags. When the bird takes
the bait, the hook catches in its throat, when it jerks its head
the stone falls off the stake, holds its head under water, and
drowns it.

Catching Frogs for Bait

Go to a spot close to the water where there are plenty of
reeds and rushes, or where the ground is littered with stones
or fallen sheets of bark. Light a little fire and let the smoke
drift through the reeds or over the stones or bark. As soon
as they smell the smoke the frogs will leave their hiding places
and hop for the water; catching them is merely a matter of
getting between them and the water, and grabbing them as
they go past.

Luring Wild Ducks

You should take up a position on the shore of the lagoon or
swamp without alarming the ducks in any way. Keep behind
cover, slap your hand upon your thigh to imitate the flapping
of a wing, grasp your nose between finger and thumb at
intervals, and imitate the nasal "k'wark, k'wark, k'wark" of a
duck. It is very difficult to give a convincing imitation of a
duck call unless the nose is held. By adopting this trick it is
possible to entice the ducks within easy shooting range.

Wildfowl Eggs

Swans nest in swampy country, choosing reeds and rushes
or on little islets. Ducks nest in hollow trees or on top of high
stumps; sometimes in clumps of rushes. Don't smash a lot
of eggs trying to find fresh ones; cut a hole in a bit of bark the
exact size of an egg and "candle" them by holding against the
sun; when there are only a few eggs in the nest, mark them
with a bit of mud and come back in a day or two to pick those
laid since your last visit.

Tough Meat

The meat of many of our native birds and animals can be
very tough unless hung for a day or two, which is out of the

question if you have nothing with which to protect it from the flies; in many cases you have to use it right away. You should pound it with the back of your bayonet on a smooth. flat stone or hard fallen log, until it is a mass of shreds. Then brown it on a flat stone which has been heated in the fire or in a dry mess tin, before adding it to a stew; or you can mix the shredded meat with chopped vegetables or biscuit crumbs and fry as a rissole.

Locating Wild Bee Hives

Take some harmless white powder, such as flour or chalk. and on a bright, sunny day, when the bees are working on the flowers or are getting water from the edge of a waterhole, dust this powder on the bees. Thus whitened, their flight can easily be followed and will lead you to the nest. Never attempt the job to get the honey on a cold day; pick a warm one. Dress in clothing with a smooth surface; don't wear anything woolly which will entangle the feet of the bees and anger them. Over your hat put a veil of old mosquito netting, tucked well into the neck of the shirt. Get your smoke fire of rolled bagging or a tin of dried manure going before you start chopping. Strain the honey from the smashed combs by putting them in a bit of clean hessian and twist it up.

Carrying a Firestick

It may be necessary to carry fire from one spot to another Get two sticks of dry, sound wood about two feet long; get one end of each burning well, take them both in the hand with

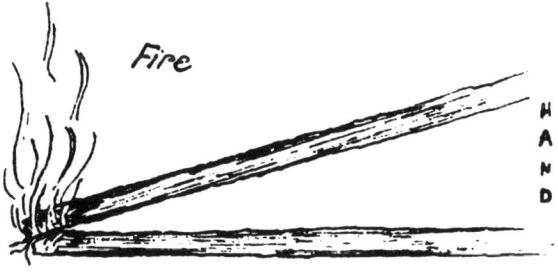

Fig. 13. CARRYING FIRE STICKS

the burning ends in contact, and as you walk along, wave the burning ends to and fro. Very seldom, and then only with a specially good burning wood such as gidgee, can a single stick be kept alight over a long distance; with two sticks in contact it is easy.

Importance of Salt

Salt in the diet is especially important in hot climates. Your body cannot perspire to cool the skin unless you have a certain amount of salt in your blood stream; if this salt is sweated out of your system and is not replaced, it brings about weakness and giddiness, followed by a complete blackout — a condition which has come to be known as "stoker's collapse." You should always carry with you a small tin of salt — a boot polish tin is about the right size — and in hot weather you should add about a quarter of a teaspoon of it to your water bottle. Salt tablets are far more convenient to carry, but you may not always have them.

Edible Seaweed

Edible seaweed is found on many parts of the coast, especially after rough weather. It is a waxy yellow colour, the stems are about a quarter of an inch in diameter, of an irregular thickness and somewhat lumpy in appearance, with touches of red, especially where the branchlets fork. Wash and dry it; it will shrink to a small bulk. To use it, soak in several lots of fresh water for 12 hours, boil a handful in a pint of water, add sugar and, if possible, a teaspoon of limejuice or a limejuice tablet. Put aside to cool; it will set into a very good jelly.

A Final Word

This booklet does not cover the subject; it is only the kindergarten primer. Bushcraft is a trade which has to be learned and learned thoroughly. You must carry on from where this book leaves off; always use your eyes to see, note and observe. The difference between the good bushman and the ordinary man is that the latter sees about one-tenth of the things about him, while the former, like the aborigine, doesn't miss much. You use your mind as a storehouse for all the information you gather against the day when it may be needed. Many of

Fig. 14. SEA WEED. ACTUAL SIZE.

the stunts mentioned in this book are much easier in theory than in practice, so never neglect an opportunity to gain proficiency by trying them out for yourself.

Everything in this book has been tried out thoroughly in the field during the past three years and any man of average intelligence can master them all if he really wants to learn.

Arbuckle Waddell Pty. Ltd.

Notes:

Notes:

Notes:

Notes:

3912153R00032

Printed in Great Britain
by Amazon.co.uk, Ltd.,
Marston Gate.